THE KINGDOM DECREE

SILFORD EDWARDS

The Kingdom Decree
Trilogy Christian Publishers A Wholly Owned Subsidiary
of Trinity Broadcasting Network
2442 Michelle Drive Tustin, CA 92780
Copyright © 2022 by Silford Edwards

All scripture quotations are taken from the King James Version of the Bible. Public domain.

Manufactured in the United States of America
10 9 8 7 6 5 4 3 2 1
Library of Congress Cataloging-in-Publication Data is available.
ISBN: 978-1-68556-486-5
E-ISBN: 978-1-68556-487-2

TABLE OF
CONTENTS

Preface

We have been called to a purpose greater than ourselves. Without people there are no nations and without God neither people or nations would exist.

As people created uniquely, our existence is deeply engraved on the sands of time as we journey throughout this life and thereafter. We are all created equal, we all share the same rights to coexist and to love, to be at peace, to experience happiness and to serve God, the creator of all things.

Our individual ideal and accomplishments should not be the benchmark to determine our level of importance to each other. We are on the same journey to embrace the essence of the glory of God and to carry out His will, which is the purpose of our lives on earth. Our purposes and paths may be different, but this pool of talents, gifts, and creativity causes us to be here at this moment.

As we stand as citizens of the Kingdom of God in one accord demonstrating the full authority of God's Kingdom on earth, let our lives reflect that which is in heaven, let's embrace the thoughts and express the action of forgiveness, and take dominion over the kingdom of darkness through prayer, praise, and covenant relationship; only then can we truly begin to heal, break curses, and live a life ordain by God. Walking in victory knowing who we are and whose we are.

We are all hurt and feel the pain of betrayal, bitterness, and disappointment in one way or the other. But if we give the power of forgiveness the opportunity to flow through our veins and heal our soul then we will see a greater tomorrow.

Let us not be ignorant of the fact that evil exist in our nations, but I say this today that the burden of hatred is too heavy, so let's choose love.

With love comes the magnitude of grace and with grace the trees of the field flourishes.

So great is the presence of God in nature that the plants, animals, fishes in the seas and oceans, and the birds in the sky all sing their praises.

If we as Kingdom citizens united for the purpose of love and shared responsibility with each other, I can assure you we will reach the mountain's top and see the beauty of the valley. As the stream flows between the mountains and supply nature with its substance let us share the love and gratitude towards our fellow human being. Let us come into the realization of who God is and our importance of Him executing His will on earth through us. Let us stand and walk in the true purpose of His will and take dominion on earth to expand His Kingdom.

To this day it is being proven that we are all here

temporarily and there are no superior people, creed, class, nor nation. Instead, we are a people created by God to share and live in unison and to worship in obedience and reverence.

Let this day be for you as for me a new day and a new path that will guide us as a people despite our culture, nation, or individual ideals. Let us dance to the universal language of love as its rhythm beat on the table of our heart.

Powerless, faithless, prayerless, and ungodlessness. Is to bring home or place emphasis on the importance of these in a believer life and the negative effect it if have if not applied to our daily lives. Thinking big! The ideology behind the popular belief that to have dominion over the kingdom of darkness concerning our lives comes with a calculative formula like quantum physics and specially crafted strategies is erroneous.

For centuries this practice has morphed itself in Christendom through religious leaders fashioning themselves as living by the principles of the Kingdom of God while having only a form of godliness but denying the power and demonstration of God. Sadly, most of us were once a part of this system. Only a few independent thinkers that truly love God and His son Jesus Christ and desire much more than a good sermon and strategic illustrations tune into the Bible, which is the word of God. It takes an understanding of the Bible to realize the level of madness being taught in the churches today, turning most churches into synagogues of Satan.

Being shocked and bamboozled of this revelation, I made an un-uttered deafening sound of awe. I know now that the Kingdom of God has so much power and the Kingdom is within us. Only if we know and apply the word of God, which is the only will of God for our lives, will the earth reflect the design of heaven, thus giving Satan no authority over us because the presence of God precludes the presence of Satan.

By this you may be wondering how some churches differ in the messages made to the people? Let me give you a brief overview of some keywords that you should take into deep consideration when carefully analysing the word of God. This will give you a better understanding of this book.

Ethnocentrisms – This has to do with customs, norms, values, and beliefs, all of which are associated with culture which is the driving force of a society. And within these societies comes governance, groups, and subgroups. What am I getting at? Religion was born out of these same patterns and is designed carefully by its members. The members establish laws to govern its culture. If these laws are not followed there is punishment, but following these laws produces rewards. Follow me: From creation God has called a set of people giving them the same establish rules or laws. But from the fall of Adam until now, humans always have deviant behaviour, although it is thought that deviant behavior brings change, regardless of whether it is good or bad. It has been proven time and time again that if we know the word of God and obey Him totally, we have automatic dominion over the kingdom of darkness. To do otherwise is death, both physically and spiritually—the latter of which is the worst. As was illustrated in the Bible the conquest of Canon, God demonstrated His love, anger, compassion, and patience to his chosen people, which Moses was the leader and out of which came this great movement. In redesigning the nation of Israel from being a polytheistic nation (many gods), a custom forced upon Israel by the rulers of Egypt, to a monotheistic nation (one God) the creator of all things gave Moses a set of laws to govern and shape the nation. These laws are the ten commandments, which were meant to guide the people. In the context of the laws there can be change giving a situation or context but the commandment changes not. God said before He changed His word heaven and earth will pass because He honors His word above His name.

Dogmatism – This is the tendency to lay down principles as incontrovertibly true, without consideration of additional evidence or the opinions of others. Please consider the word "incontrovertible."

The Marriam-Webster dictionary defines dogmatism as the expression of an opinion or belief as if it were a fact; positiveness in assertion of opinion especially when unwarranted or arrogant; a viewpoint or system of ideas based on insufficient examined premises.

Now to link the word "incontrovertible" to a positiveness in assertion of opinion and the viewpoint of a system is the very reason why the church has become a cliché having only a form of godliness but denying the power thereof. God the creator of all things is now a subjective being in the mind of people to fit in a belief system. We see the use of crafted words and bylaws to educate a people based on their own incontrovertible opinion and the use of a spirit of positiveness to hide the truth of God to gain the overall objective of a system instead of the will of God. Hence the word "perversion."

Perversion – The alteration of something from its original course, meaning, or state to a distortion or corruption of what was first intended.

It is said that "all great evil is the perversion of a good." Synonyms: distortion, misrepresentation, falsification, travesty, misinterpretation, misconstruction, twisting, corruption, subversion, misuse.

What am I saying? Each word has two meanings: (1) a denotative meaning, which is a broad definition, (2) a connotative meaning, which uses the context the word to determine tone. The biblical context of 'perversion' amplifies numerous sorts to which there are recompense. Fashioning in our society today is the greatest sin—the perversion of God's words. The book of Deuteronomy Chapter 28 highlights the blessings of obedience and rewards for perversion of His word. I invite you to examine your lives or those of others. I almost guarantee that you can identify what I am saying. It speaks for itself.

Curses – A solemn utterance intended to invoke a supernatural power to inflict harm or punishment on someone or something.

The act of perversion of the word of God brings curses on our lives in different ways. It all depends on the type and level. The only weapon that can be used against us is your own disobedience. Satan's evil has no power over good. Curses can only be broken from our lives when we identify and acknowledge them and then apply the blood of Jesus Christ through prayer, the word, and faith. The question now is, can a born-again child of God be under a curse? The answer to that question has two parts to which I will explain. Legally a Christian cannot be under a curse but experientially it is possible. The death resurrection of Christ will free believers from the law of sin and death will allow the word of God to transform our lives because the blood of Jesus Christ has paid the price.

Curses operate in the bloodline, meaning from generation to generation. This may be a result of sins committed by our distant ancestors or even immediate parents. When those sins were committed, it opened doors for demonic or satanic spirits to enter the bloodline giving them the legal rights to operate in our lives. Having those legal rights, the demonic spirits move from one person to the next of the same bloodline carrying its duty to destroy and making our lives full of misfortunes. For example, terminal illness, poverty, bad luck, setback, brokenness, mental illness just to name a few. If there is a curse operating in your bloodline becoming a Christian does not stop the evil spirit from operating in your life causing you to face some of the challenges daily.

To stop the experiential effects generational curses have on our lives we must first identify the legal rights those demonic spirits are operating under in the believer life. After identifying the legal right these entities are operating under, as people with the anointing and gifting of the Holy Spirit, we administer deliverance through the blood of Jesus Christ and command those demons to leave a person's life. After which the believer will start have new experiences. Deliverance is needed in the life of believers to break generational curses. After all, deliverance is for believers and not unbelievers because the Bible stated if we administer deliverance to an unbeliever the demons will leave and come back to reposes the unbeliever. If the demons find the 'house' (which is the person's body) clean, the demons will go and invite other demons, more dangerous than themselves, to make the person worse. Why? Because only the word and spirit of

God can save and protect you from these forces. If you don't have a covenant relationship with God, you do not have that spiritual authority. It is important to come to Christ.

This scripture is a clear indication that believers can be under a curse. God made special provisions through His blood to protect us from generational demonic influence that seems to inevitably cause problems in our lives.

Prayer – A solemn request for help or expression of thanks addressed to God.

Prayer is the most fundamentals weapon in a Christian's life. To be an effective warrior requires in-depth knowledge of the words and things of God. One must also develop and maintain a close relationship with him by not perverting or disobeying His word. Furthermore, we must also know that the word of God is the only will for our lives. Therefore, when praying, applying the written words of God makes our request become unhindered and to ensure absolute results. Jesus Christ demonstrated this by teaching His disciples to pray.

Who is this book for?

The contents of this book were written specifically for all those who feel they miserably fail themselves, friends, loved ones, and God. This is for anyone who has suffered the consequences of sin and is living a life of poverty, oppression, suppression, depression, or abortion of destiny. To the brother or sister that is a slave to iniquity and the never-ending cycle of presumptuous evil and heaven seems to shut the door on them. To the sick that cannot be healed or the captive that cannot be set free. Those that are living under generational curses are paying the price for sins they knew nothing about. To those that truly love God and want to live a life in Him but struggle by the ever presence of evil designed to destroy them. To those who want to but cannot pray and that just need a new inspiration to fight. To the weak. Letting you know that your strength is in the Lord not self. As you read, if you can be identified with any of these, the volume of this book is for you.

1. Have you ever prayed, and it seemed like God did not care to listen or even care to answer your request?
2. Is there any identifiable cycle of defeat in your life?
3. What about prayerlessness? Do you find it hard to pray? Or do you find that you have not prayed in

a while?

4. Do you know the importance of prayer and the positive effect it has on you as a person?

This book will speak to all areas of your life and can be used as a guide in your quest to becoming the better you.

This honoured inception came as a result of major challenges I encountered in my life. These difficult times brought me closer to God through Jesus Christ. My newly developed thirst for answers to my situation has opened doors to which I was exposed to and gained significant knowledge in the area of prayer, spiritual warfare, generational curses, and how to break demonic attacks. For years we have worked both as a team and on an individual basis to carry out the work of the Kingdom of God and the demonstration of His power and authority over satanic operations. As my experience grew in faith I started to learn about strategic prayer and the dynamics of praying the words of God from the Bible, the promises, blessings, affirmations, authority, and most importantly the love of God. Having gained these experiences it is only right to teach others to apply these principles to their lives so that they can become more effective in prayer and their overall development in the things concerning the Kingdom of God.

Reflective thoughts and expressions

Personal notes: _____

_____

_____

_____

_____

_____

_____

_____

_____

_____

_____

_____

_____

_____

_____

_____

_____

_____

_____

_____

_____

_____

Acknowledgement

I first give thanks to God the Father. Through His Son, Jesus Christ, and His leading guidance, inspired me with knowledge of the Holy Spirit. My dearest dedication is to my daughter Heavenleigh Malier-Edwards who God has used to remind me of the simple fact that He is in control. He has proved Himself to me from her miraculous conception, the almost aborted destiny, the journey through formation in the womb, the almost untimely exit from the womb, the countless encounters until now. Her life inspires me to build my faith in God through Jesus Christ living each day asking for today's bread. These trying times give birth to this book. My deepest gratitude with sentiments goes to all beautiful people in my life that are the driving forces behind me completing this book and sharing it with the world. Their understanding and devotion for the things of God is unspeakable. To my production team, marketing, sales, and distribution networks, to the reader and sharer of this book, I must say a big thanks to you. And may the Lord bless you and keep you and cause His face to shine on you and give you peace. Selah!

Reflective thoughts and expressions

Personal notes: _____

_____

_____

_____

_____

_____

_____

_____

_____

_____

_____

_____

_____

_____

_____

_____

_____

_____

_____

_____

_____

Introduction

It is my greatest desire that this volume will bring you to the realization that within yourself lies the power of the Kingdom of God. And this glory, dominion, and authority are all given to you as tools and weapon of warfare to expand God's Kingdom on earth. There will be a greater understanding of the power of God through strategic praying, the demonstration of the power of God. This little book consists of some of the most powerful and weaponized prayers at different levels of warfare from forgiveness, praise, and deliverance to destroying the work and camp of the enemy. You will be exposed to and gain significant knowledge in spiritual warfare and have a better understanding of how to overcome difficult situations we may face daily. I know that after developing a prayerful life you will never be the same. Your life will be transformed to one which reflects the Kingdom of God on earth.

Reflective thoughts and expressions

Personal notes: _____

_____

_____

_____

_____

_____

_____

_____

_____

_____

_____

_____

_____

_____

_____

_____

_____

_____

_____

_____

_____

_____

Chapter 1

The Kingdom Explained

I am almost certain in one way or the other you have heard the term "Kingdom of God" be used either to explain or justify the word or work of God in the present world or the one to come. This over exaggeration of the term in a dogmatized manner without the full demonstration of the authority and power of God on earth has left most of us with little or no belief if this Kingdom really exists. On the contrary, God has created this earth and given us full dominion. Since this expression of spiritual authority and Kingdom lifestyle is not the norm in our societies today, it is likely that we have somehow forgotten the basic principles that is required to walk in the presence of God and to effectively fulfil our lives on earth.

The greatest definition about the Kingdom of God I have heard is that the Kingdom realm is not a geographical location but a dimension behind human existence. And it is not controlled by time, space, or matter. It is for this reason time, space, and matter were created simultaneously. This demonstration shows us that it takes a greater power and authority outside of this earthly realm to bring them into existence. The question is does God really exists? Yes. And was He created? No.

Entering this dimension is not impossible, but it takes understanding, commitment, and a deliberate decision on our path to let thy will be done in our lives. Throughout time it is evident in the Bible and other historical documentations that God has always dealt with mankind through covenant relationship. This is important because according to the Bible, we were all born in the state of sin, not by choice but by the very nature of our stead. As mentioned in Romans 3:10, "As it is written: There is none that is righteous, no, not one." And in the book of Isaiah 64:6, "But we are all as an unclean thing, and all our righteousness are as filthy rags; and we all do fade as a leaf; and our iniquities, like the wind, have taken us away."

Notice Roman 3:10 uses the words "as it is written." This means that there is already a conclusion of the state of us as humans, and it will take something outside of our existence to reconcile us with God. This is called a covenant.

What is a covenant? It is the legally binding agreement, whether spiritually or naturally, between human beings or God and man. This agreement comes with certain requirements to be carried out by both parties in order to achieve a mutually beneficial result. This covenant is governed by laws outside of the agreement that can be used to bring conclusion in terms of rewards or punishment if either party decided to breach the terms of the covenant or agreement. Therefore, to enter into the Kingdom of God requires us to enter into and maintain a covenant relationship with God through Christ.

The Kingdom of God is not pluralistic but rather inclusive. We hold firm to the belief that there is only one God the creator of all things, Jesus Christ His only begotten Son, and the Holy spirit, each having their individual functions but operating as one with the same essence and nature. Jesus makes mention of their primary functions as the Father sent Jesus, and when Jesus goes He will send us the Holy Spirit to comfort us. In the book of Matthew 28:19 when Jesus said this: "Go ye therefore, and teach all nations, baptizing them in the name of the Father, and of the Son, and of the Holy Ghost."

This a clear indication that the character of God functions as three distinct entity inseparables with the same essence and nature. Some call it the "Trinity."

Base on this fundamental belief, we recognize that we all have sinned and come short of the glory, forgiveness, and mercy of God.

Reflective thoughts and expressions

1. What do you understand so far about this book? _____

_____

_____

_____

_____

_____

_____

Personal notes: _____

_____

_____

_____

_____

_____

_____

_____

_____

_____

_____

_____

_____

Chapter 2

The Lord's Prayer Explained

The Lord's Prayer as we know it is way more advanced and detailed than we literally take it. These words were carefully crafted and strategically structured by Jesus Christ, the master builder, that when unfolded speaks to every area of your lives, His glory, His love, and His willingness to grant us your requests if we follow the set structure. In addition, God's greatest desire is to have the Kingdom of heaven be reflected on earth. This prayer lays out in steps, or what we call prayer points, to be used when praying. An example of which will be illustrated.

"Our Father which art in heaven, Hallowed be thy name. Thy kingdom come, Thy will be done in earth, as it is in heaven" (Matthew 6:9-10).

Remember these words? The first lines of the prayer deal with the following characteristics of God: His Lordship; His sovereignty or His ability to govern and to enforce His will on earth; His holiness, reverence, and awesomeness; and His intention to make earth and our lives a reflection of what He established in heaven.

When praying one must acknowledge these characteristics of God making mention of them. After all, identifying who you are praying to is the only assurance of an unhindered request. For example:

Prayer:

Father in the name of Jesus, you are God. Above all we worship you because you are King of kings. Hallowed be your name. As you said, your Kingdom come, your will be done on earth as it is in heaven. Lord, let your will be done in my life. Let my life be a reflection of your Kingdom. For in your Kingdom no principalities can exist, and the gate of hell is defeated. Therefore, I stand on the authority of the sovereign Lord, and I declare that the Kingdom of God will be established in my life now. Amen.

"Give us this day our daily bread" (Matthew 6:11). Specificity is one of the traits most humans lack. However, when it comes to the things of God, especially prayer request, we must have clearly defined purpose and a desired outcome. We must also be willing to be concise and precise. When Christ mentioned 'bread,' He was not literally talking about something to eat only. But the broader aspect of life and everything needed for it to function as designed. Let us pray.

Prayer

God, in your word you said that we must seek you first and that when I ask, I will receive, when I knock, the doors will be opened and when I seek your face, I will find it. Now, God, today I ask that you give me my daily bread. I seek not tomorrow's bread, Lord. But I need a financial breakthrough because you said in your word that the righteous will not be forsaken neither will their seed beg bread. Based on the authority you gave me when I received the mark of your blood, Jesus, I command a supernatural blessing for myself and my generation to come. I declare that the kingdom of darkness will not hinder my breakthrough. In Jesus' name, amen.

"And forgive us our debts, as we forgive our debtors" (Matthew 6:12).

Many Christians lose their way because of lack of forgiveness. God says that if we don't forgive those that do us wrong, He will not show us forgiveness. Before we ask for His mercies, we must first be merciful. We must forgive.

Prayer

Father, in the name of Jesus who died on the cross for my sins, I ask that you give me a heart of forgiveness. Jesus, search me and see if there are any wicked ways

in me and cleanse me. In that light I ask for your mercy,
Lord. In your words you said that the blood of your son
Jesus will wash me clean and purify me and make me a
vessel of honour. In Jesus' name, amen.

"And lead us not into temptation, but deliver us
from evil" (Matthew 6:13).

Throughout life most of us believe that we cannot
avert temptation. But in the Lord's Prayer, Jesus Christ
specifically asked God, His father, not to lead us into
temptation. Therefore, we can pray and ask God to remove the possibility of temptation before it happens so
we can focus on building a life for the Kingdom of God.

Prayer

Father Lord, this moment I petition your throne know-
ing that without you I cannot make it through this life. So
I ask, oh Lord, that you remove from my path all possibil-
ities of temptation now and in the future. In your words
you said your words are a lamp unto my feet and a light
unto my path. This day as I walk let my steps be ordered
by you, let my mind and everything I do be pleasing to
you, Lord, because I know that your Spirit lives in me and
is greater than anyone that lives in this world. Amen.

"For thine is the Kingdom, and the power, and the glory, for ever. Amen" (Matthew 6:13).

As in the beginning of the prayer it speaks of His power and awesomeness it ends with the same authority. This means that whenever you pray the words of God a seal is placed on those words that Satan cannot interfere. And that seal is the blood of Christ.

Now that you understand the fundamental principle of prayer, I can now teach you how to position yourself to war against the kingdom of darkness from a place of victory.

Reflective thoughts and expressions

Personal notes: _____

_____

_____

_____

_____

_____

_____

_____

_____

_____

_____

_____

_____

_____

_____

_____

_____

_____

_____

_____

_____

_____

_____

Chapter 3

Preparing for Battle

Keynote

Before taking on any spiritual warfare, one must first understand the authority and the scope in which to operate. Spiritual warfare requires a certain level of spiritual maturity that will help us to overcome demonic powers, influences, and retaliations. Within the volume of this book as I layout different prayer points for different spiritual attacks I am encouraging you to carefully read these notes before you begin and know when to apply them.

Importantly, although the Bible speaks of deliverance and healing, one cannot be totally free from these demonic powers until you surrender your life totally to Christ. According to the Bible, deliverance is for believers and salvation is for unbelievers. When an unbeliever is delivered from a demonic influence, that demon leaves the person then returns with seven other demons more devious than itself. If when it return the house or person in not filled with the Spirit of God then the demons re-enter that person making them worse than before as is seen in Matthew 12:43-45. Therefore, it is advisable to teach salvation to the lost and administer deliverance when they come to Christ. There are times when God will instruct us to demonstrate His power to bring home a point to unbelievers for His glory.

PRAYERS OF RENUNCIATION AND ACTIVATION

Before taking on any spiritual battle, one must first make sure that there are no identifiable sins within. It means repentance for believers is continuous; we must ask God to forgive us of our sins known and unknown and to wash us clean with the blood of Jesus Christ. If there are any instances of identifiable sins in us, we will not have the spiritual authority to command the demons to set people free. This level of warfare is serious and cannot be taken lightly. Each line below is a complete prayer topic or prayer point.

Prayer of Repentance

1. Father, in the name of Jesus Christ I ask for your forgiveness from sin.
2. Your word said in Psalm 103:10-12 that you have not dealt with us according to our sins, nor punished us according to our iniquities.
3. But for as the heavens are high above the earth, so great is your mercy towards those who fear you.
4. We thank you, Lord, that the blood of Jesus cleanse us from all unrighteousness.
5. And as far as the east is from the west, so far as you will remove our transgression from us if we ask and believe.

33

6. We thank you Lord for your mercies, compassion, and love towards us.

7. As Psalm 51 clearly states, you require a broken heart but not sacrifice of animals.

8. We believe and know that you send your son Jesus Christ to be the ultimate sacrifice for us.

9. His death, resurrection, and ascension to glory give us hope that you shall return to gather your people.

10. All knees shall bow and every tongue shall confess that you are Lord.

11. Father, we thank you for your forgiveness and mercies on us.

12. Deliver us from him that is too strong for us and give us strength to overcome the traps of Satan. In Jesus' matchless name.

13. To any sins hiding in any part of our bodies, minds, and spirits, we command you take your flight now and leave.

14. As the word of God says in Acts 3:19, "Repent ye therefore, and be converted, that your sins may be blotted out, when the times of refreshing shall come from the presence of the Lord."

15. We thank you Lord for your forgiveness and mercies and ask that as we declare your word that it will go forth and accomplish thy will in our life and on earth. We thank you for hearing our prayers. Amen.

Reflective thoughts and expressions

What have you learned about the importance of repentance? _____

_____

_____

_____

_____

_____

How does this prayer impact your prayer life? _____

_____

_____

_____

_____

Personal notes: _____

_____

_____

_____

_____

_____

_____

_____

_____

_____

_____

The Lord enthrone on the praise of His people. Giving God praise is vital in spiritual warfare. During praise, there will be manifestation of demons because evil cannot dwell in the presence of God. The word of the Lord said in Psalm 91:10, "There shall no evil befall thee, neither shall any plague come nigh thy dwelling." Let us lift the praise to the highest through His son, Jesus Christ.

Prayer of Praise

1. From everlasting to everlasting, you are God alone, and there is no one mightier than you.
2. The heavens and the earth were created by you; the stars, suns, moons, rivers, seas, and mountains were established when you spoke.
3. I thank you that I was created in your own image, oh, God.
4. You are the God of Abraham, Isaac, Joseph. You sent your only begotten son, Jesus Christ, to die for us. Your love is everlasting.
5. You establish great kings; your voice divides the wilderness.
6. The Lord shakes the wilderness of Kadesh.
7. You sat enthroned upon the floods.
8. I will worship you in the beauty of your holiness.
9. Your voice is powerful; your voice is full of majesty.

10. I worship you alone.

11. You are the God of the heavenly host. All angels bow down and worship you.

12. You are higher than the highest and mightier than the mightiest. You are greater than the seas. You are the all time undefeated champion that reigns forever and ever. Amen.

A Call to Worship (inspired by Psalm 95)

1. Let us worship the Lord and sing a new song unto the Lord of heavenly hosts.

2. Shout for joy, all the people, to the rock of our salvation. Praise His name. Selah!

3. In your presence, I will come with thanksgiving.

4. I will be joyful and shout and sing the psalms to you.

5. For you, oh Lord, are the great God of all times. I magnify your name in all the earth.

6. You hold the foundation and the deep places of the earth in your hands.

7. The heights of the hills are yours, also.

8. You made the seas, and your hands form the dry land.

9. I will worship and bow down to you in awe for you are the great God of creation.

10. And I will kneel to you, oh Lord my maker, for you are God.

11. I command my will to serve you and my heart to follow after you

12. In the mornings I will worship you. Great is thy faithfulness, oh Lord.

13. Blessing and glory and power and dominion to you for ever and ever. Amen.

Section 2

PRAYERS OF DELIVERANCE

Self-deliverance is very important in spiritual warfare because you must be at a place of renewed strength and power to deal with these devils. So, put on the whole armour of God in this time and break free from these evil plots.

Self-deliverance; breaking free from iniquity:

1. To the lover of our souls, the father of creation who sent His son, Jesus Christ, hollowed be thy name.
2. You have created us in your own image, and you have made us your joint heir through the blood of Jesus Christ.
3. You said in your words in the book of Matthew 18:18, "Verily I say unto you, Whatsoever ye shall bind on earth shall be bound in heaven: and whatsoever ye shall loose on earth shall be loosed (sic) in heaven."

4. We call on this authority with the anointing you gave us, Lord, and we speak to the atmosphere beneath our feet and above our heads, we command you to stop all assignments against us set by evil.

5. We reverse every assignment given to any demonic realm to supervise our life. Let the finger of God blind them. In Jesus' name.

6. "For I will cleanse their blood that I have not cleansed: for the LORD dwelleth in Zion" (Joel 3:21).

7. Oh Lord, rain fire, lightening and affliction upon the marine spirits that are set up to destroy our destinies. We rebuke you in Jesus' name.

8. To every satanic trap from the sun working against our life and families, the Lord rebukes you and casts you down.

9. For the sun shall not smite us by day. We command you this moment, lift away your warfare from our life now and never return. In the name of Jesus.

10. We speak to every working of the moon. Shut up your light from night raiders, because they shall not smite us.

11. We break to pieces the hidden arrow of wickedness. Come out now by fire and return to sender. Destroy them now. In the name of Jesus.

12. Evil powers of enchantment against our life and

families, we command your bellies to be bitter. Get out. In the name of Jesus.

13. Moon, sun, and stars, holding any enchantment against our lifes and families, in the name of Jesus, release us.

14. We command the earth in the name of Jesus to open wide your gates and release every wickedness set against our life and burn the root of every evil plant that had been planted in our life and families. In the mighty name of Jesus Christ.

15. We take the axe of God which is the word and we place it at the root of every evil root in our life and families to cut it down.

16. The fire of God visits our life and families and burns all evil roots until they are utterly destroyed.

17. Let your holy fire and power, oh Lord, break every yoke of iniquity upon our life. Scatter and destroy them forever. In the name of Jesus.

18. Throne of witchcraft established over our life and families, I command you to overturn now and burn by the fire of God.

19. Let the east wind blow and scatter beyond redemption their ashes.

20. We ask this moment that you send your angel Michael on our behalf against the prince of darkness and chase them until they are defeated.

21. Visit our bloodlines with fire, vengeance, the

sword, and the blood of Jesus Christ. Cut off all ties and generational curses operating in our life and families by the power of Jesus Christ.

22. We put our family and self under the shadow of your wings. Let no evil befall us. Neither let any plague come near our dwellings. Deliver us from them that are too strong for us.

23. We command deliverance from all spirit of bondage released against our life and families now. In Jesus Christ's name, amen.

Destroying evil satanic plots set against us:

1. The wisdom of God surpasses all human understanding. In creation you breathe life in us, and we became living souls.

2. Because of your love for us, you sent Jesus Christ your only begotten son to die and pay the ultimate price for our sins to bring us back to you.

3. We thank you and bless your holy name forever and ever. Amen.

4. With this love of God and the power of the blood of Jesus Christ we decree.

5. No weapon formed against us shall prosper. We break every witchcraft plot that seeks to establish itself over our life and families, business and church, and everything concerning us. In the name

of Jesus.

6. And now, let every evil plot be shared out to them that desire our harm and in the very destruction let them fall. Let the blood of Jesus Christ and fire consume them now.

7. Psalm 35:1-2, "Plead my cause, O Lord, with them that strive with me: fight against them that fight against me. Take hold of shield and buckler, and stand up for mine help."

8. We ask the spirit of God to blind every evil eye seeking out our affairs. In the name of Jesus.

9. To the spirit of witchcraft assignments working against us, we bring the judgment of God on you, and we pray that your plans will be defeated. In the mighty name of Jesus.

10. As it is written in 2 Corinthians 10:4, "For the weapons of our warfare are not carnal, but mighty through God to the pulling down of strong holds."

11. We command darkness seated against our life be exposed by the light and fire of God.

12. Every wicked tongue that rises against us and evil power calling our names into any plots or destruction, fall and die. In the mighty name of Jesus Christ.

13. All wickedness working against our progress, receive the fire of judgment. Vengeance is the Lord's not ours.

14. Every satanic plot and demonic scheme emanating from the pit of hell and darkness, be reversed. In the name of Jesus.

15. We disentangle ourselves and our families from every witchcraft trap. In the name of Jesus.

16. We command every evil and concoction used against our life to break to pieces. In the name of Jesus.

17. Lord, by your awesome power, keep our souls and deliver us from the clutches of Satan.

18. Let confusion rain upon the heads of them that plot our harm and downfall.

19. We command every spirit working against us to stop, turn, and war with each other now. In the mighty name of Jesus.

20. Let the gates of hell be shut and all demons causing problems in my life be tormented until that Day of Judgment. Amen.

Prayer Against Occult Burial:

1. Isaiah 8:10 says, "Take counsel together, and it shall come to nought; speak the word, and it shall not stand: for God is with us."

2. We speak to the earth and ask that the spirit of God go down and destroy all wickedness buried against us by our enemies. In the name of Jesus

Christ.

3. Psalm 49:15 says, "But God will redeem my soul from the power of the grave: for he shall receive me. Selah." Let the spirit of God break and destroy all witchcraft burials and any holds it may have on my life. In Jesus' name.

4. Let the spirit of God reverse every witchcraft burial and occult practices in our life and families, oh mighty God.

5. Every witchcraft burial working against us, we cut you off and command you to be reversed now. In the name of Jesus.

6. We called with authority all burial against our finances, business, and everything concerning our life. We command you to give up what belongs to us now. In the name of Jesus.

7. Now, nullify the power of witchcraft burial against our progress now.

8. We speak to all blessings imprisoned by the grave, come forth in the name of Jesus.

9. We lose our blessings from the hands of the dead. In the name of Jesus.

10. Anything that has been done against us using the ground, be neutralized. In the name of Jesus.

11. We command and pluck up all evil deeds planted on earth against our life and family. In Jesus' name.

12. We slay every demon operating under the earth for evil purpose with the sword of God.
13. Let earthquakes shake Satan out of his setting and expose him to the fire of God.
14. And now we command the earth to bring forth fruits of blessings in our life and the all-healing herbs. In Jesus Christ's name, amen.

Cancelling Negative Words Spoken Over My Life: Every negative word spoken over our lives must be broken for us to fulfil our destiny.

1. According to the book of Proverbs 18:21, "Death and life are in the power of the tongue: and they that love it shall eat the fruit thereof."
2. In the name of Jesus Christ, son of the living God who is the creator of all things, I wecome in your presence, knowing that we were made in your own image, and you breathe the breath of life in us.
3. We have sinned and come short of your glory, and we repented and were forgiven.
4. We meditate on your words both day and night and our delight is in your law, oh Lord. As in the

book of Psalm 1:2.

5. You said in Psalm 1:3, "And he shall be like a tree planted by the rivers of water, that bringeth forth his fruit in his season; his leaf also shall not wither; and whatsoever he doeth shall prosper." We thank you for using "shall" in your words. It means the future from this time forth and forever more.

6. We cancel by fire all negative words spoken against our life and my families. Let them melt like wax at the presence of God.

7. Spirit of God, locate all stubborn demons of infirmity and destiny killers and deliver us from them by your fire.

8. We command all witchcraft foundation in our life be uprooted by fire. In the name of Jesus Christ.

9. All money spent in occult activities on our behalf, we command you to burn by the fire of God.

10. We break every evil decree over our life. Let the fire of God destroy them because we are the blessings of the Lord.

11. Demon of infirmity, we cancel your effect now in our bodies. Receive the fire of God and the blood of Jesus and burn you to ashes. In Jesus' name.

12. Every monitoring spirit assigned by Satan to seek out our life, we command you to return to your sender. In the name of Jesus.

13. We speak to the spirit of bitterness issued against our life by witchcraft spirits to break your hold now. In the name of Jesus.

14. To the curse of desolation issued against our bodies by witchcraft, be broken by the blood of Jesus.

15. To the curse of miscarriages issued against our life, break by fire. We will fulfil our destiny on earth.

16. May the verdict of witchcraft be nullified now by the blood of Jesus Christ.

17. We speak the word "shall" over our life now and we decree that we are trees planted by the rivers of water. In everything we do we will prosper.

18. We decree and declare that the spirit of excellence and accomplishment will arise in us now.

19. Let the fire of God surround us and every side protect us from all negative words.

20. We thank you, Lord, for breaking us from all negative words spoken against our life. In Jesus' name, amen.

Breaking Curses:

1. Baptize us with the presence of your fire, oh God, and let the blood of Jesus cleans us from all un-righteousness.
2. Let the power of God destroy and break all witch-craft curses sent against us.
3. Now, Lord, destroy every curse that has been operating in our life by your fire.
4. You are our divine destiny; we will not be be-witched nor cursed anymore. Because we were bought with the precious blood of Jesus, we are free from all wickedness.
5. We command the spirit of witchcraft curses assigned to bring our life to an expected end to return to their sender now.
6. Let all demons scatter from our life and affairs now. May the Lord's reign chase them with fire. In the name of Jesus Christ.
7. All generational curses that cause witchcraft to enter our bloodlines through any and every form of agreement, we use the blood of Jesus to erase you from our bloodlines.
8. Cover our life and families, oh God, under the blood of Jesus Christ.
9. Hide us in the secret place of your tabernacle

and let our heads be lifted up above our enemies around about us.

10. Your word said in Psalm 23:4, "Yea, though I walk through the valley of the shadow of death, I will fear no evil: for thou art with me; thy rod and thy staff they comfort me."

11. Lord, you said in Psalm 23:5, "Thou preparest a table before me in the presence of mine enemies: thou anointest my head with oil; my cup runneth over."

12. We ask that you now break all negative words spoken against our life and families that cause a curse. In the mighty name of Jesus.

13. Lord destroy every plot that is designed to destroy our life and families.

14. Father, in the name of Jesus destroy with your word all demons assigned to block, destroy, or hinder my progress.

15. All power and dominion and strength belong to you, God the creator of all things, amen. And amen, Selah.

Destroying the Power of Witchcraft Food Eaten:

1. John 7:38 says, "He that believeth on me, as the scripture hath said, out of his belly shall flow rivers of living water."
2. Jesus Christ, we ask that you let our intestines and every organ of our bodies experience your fire and consume every evil deposit.
3. As it is written in the book of Mark 16:18, "They shall take up serpents; and if they drink any deadly thing, it shall not hurt them; they shall lay hands on the sick, and they shall recover."
4. We thank you, Lord, for that confirmation.
5. And now, let there be a disassociation between our bodies and the evil food we have eaten. Bring them out.
6. In the name of Jesus, we vomit out every evil food that we have eaten. Cleanse us totally from the remnant of them by your Holy Ghost's fire.
7. Let the healing power of the blood of Jesus flush out every poison deposited in our blood and stomach as a result of evil food. In Jesus' name.
8. Father, in the name of Jesus Christ, we ask you to restore all that we have lost as a result of eating evil food.

9. All agreement that we are in because of evil food eaten we break you with the blood of Jesus Christ. Come out of us now.

10. Blockages and abortion of destiny caused by witchcraft food eaten, we command you now by the fire of God to break and vomit out. Every last one of you. By the mighty and awesome name of Jesus Christ, get out.

11. Deliver us from the plots of this evil, oh Lord God of Israel, and rescue our souls and break now. In Jesus' name, get out of us.

12. Evil deposit, the fire and the host of heaven is against you. Die. Get out of us now. In Jesus' name.

13. Heal now the sickness caused by evil food we have eaten.

14. Demon causing sickness in our bodies because of witchcraft food we have eaten, flee from us now.

15. We renounce all soul ties, attachment vows, and commitments made as a result of witchcraft food we have eaten. Now break, set us free, get out. In the name of Jesus Christ.

16. Get out now, break. Be destroyed from our life. Our bodies, our spirits, and our souls burn you, evil deposit. In Jesus' name.

Breaking the Spirit of Infirmity From My Life:

1. Isaiah 53:5 said, "But he was wounded for our transgressions, he was bruised for our iniquities: the chastisement of our peace was upon him; and with his stripes we are healed."

2. We stand fast, therefore, in the liberty by which Christ has made us free, and will not be entangled again with a yoke of bondage.

3. We speak to every demon operating through witchcraft in our life – somersault, fall down, and die. In the name of Jesus.

4. We are healed by the stripes of Jesus Christ as was declared by the word of God.

5. "He sent his word, and healed them, and delivered them from their destructions" (Psalm 107:20). Lord, send your spirit to administer healing to our bodies.

6. We command total realignment of any part of our bodies that has been fragmented by the power of infirmity through evil. In Jesus' name.

7. "For I will restore health unto thee, and I will heal thee of thy wounds, saith the LORD" (Jeremiah 30:17).

8. We pronounce death up the power of any infirmity

working in any part of our bodies. Now, dry up, healing is mine.

9. We are the joint heir with Christ, therefore, we stand above all sickness and command all demons carrying sickness to our life to return to their sender.

10. Let destruction go to the root of any infirmity planted by witchcraft in our life and destroy it, pluck it out now in the name of Jesus.

11. Every inherited sickness from our family lineages, dry to your roots, burn and cast out. Get out, evil root of sickness.

12. "Confess your faults one to another, and pray one for another, that ye may be healed. The effectual fervent prayer of a righteous man availeth much" (James 5:16).

13. On these promises we decree and declare that we are healed. In the name of Jesus Christ, amen.

Reflective thoughts and expressions

Personal notes: _____

_____

_____

_____

_____

_____

_____

_____

_____

_____

_____

_____

_____

_____

_____

_____

_____

_____

_____

_____

_____

_____

_____

_____

Section 3

Warfare Prayers

Spiritual warfare is a direct attack on the kingdom of darkness, Satan, and his angels. This level of praying requires focus and total commitment to the will of God. To attack is different from defending or breaking on impact. Whenever you start to attack wickedness be aware that there is going to be retaliation from the dark side. If you're not prepared mentally, spiritually, and physically, don't start this warfare because your life can be destroyed. Before you engage in this type of spiritual warfare ensure you are at a place of spiritual maturity so that you can combat the kingdom of darkness. Greater anointing comes with greater responsibilities and greater authority.

War Against the Plots of Wickedness

1. In the name of Jesus Christ, we cancel every one of the enemy's plans over our life and family, now.
2. We command every evil to return to their sender

and release your arrows on them.

3. We apply the fire of God and we curse the curses sent against us. Turn them into a blessing. In the name of Jesus, change our destiny for better.

4. As the Lord God Almighty rules, let the heavens send judgment against every strange covenant of darkness. In the name of Jesus.

5. Make us an instrument of spiritual violence and a heart that hates evil.

6. Teach us how to fight and take our hands to war.

7. Let us be your battle axe against wickedness.

8. We will not sleep, and neither will we give slumber to our eyes until the wicked are destroyed.

9. Break every evil authority and every wicked word spoken by them against us. In the name of Jesus Christ.

10. As you destroy the walls of Jericho, Lord, break every dark resistance set up against us. In the name of Jesus.

11. Execute judgement on them that desire our hurt, chase them with thy tempest, defeat them, Lord.

12. There is no remembrance of you in the grave neither can we give you praise. Therefore, break the evil plots so that we can freely praise you.

13. Holy fire, break the backbones and destroy the roots of every evil spirit that is speaking against us now. In the name of Jesus.

14. Let your serpent swallow the serpent of Pharaoh working against us and cut off the head of the dragon. In the name of Jesus Christ.
15. We cast every bondage off our life, in the name of Jesus Christ.
16. Use the keys of heaven to lock out problems from our life, now. In the name of Jesus.
17. All powers given to Him in heaven and on earth. What we bind in heaven is bound and whatever we lose on earth is losed.
18. We bind the spirit of destruction operating in our life, and we lose ourself from the bond of wickedness.
19. Let the angels of God chastise them. Now lift us up lest we dash our feet against a stone.
20. The wicked shall melt at your presence and fire will consume them now. In Jesus' name, amen.

Breaking Evil from My Home

1. Our homes are homes of prayer, and it shall be so.
2. Let every presence of witchcraft in our household and life be burned by the fire of God.
3. Psalm 91:10, "There shall no evil befall thee, neither shall any plague come nigh thy dwelling."
4. Let the thunder of God scatter beyond redemption

the foundation of witchcraft in our homes and life. In Jesus' name.

5. We renounce every stronghold of evil plots that want to take refuge in our house. Be destroyed by the blood of Jesus Christ and the fire of God.

6. Lord, as we set on the alter with the sacrifice of praise let your angels ascend and descend from our homes and properties.

7. Lord, expose them that are hiding in our life and house and let their secret places burn by your fire, oh God. In Jesus' name.

8. Let every local and international satanic network setup against us and our households be shattered to pieces. In Jesus' name.

9. Release confusion on them that plot against us, and let them attack each other.

10. Fire of God, destroy every stronghold of evil that we have inherited through our bloodlines. In the name of Jesus.

11. Let the spirit of God break down and burn to ashes every high place of witchcraft stronghold that we have built with our mouths. We cancel their effects upon our life, in the name of Jesus.

12. We stand in the liberty of Christ in God, and we command all demonic forces working to destroy our houses and families to get out.

13. Lord, close every door that is open because of the

sins we have committed or those of our ancestors.

14. We go to the enemy's camp this moment and take back by force everything that was stolen from us.

15. Lord, release your angels to war in the heavens and the earth beneath on our behalf.

16. We release thunder, lightning, and fire on the marine demons now. In Jesus' name.

17. Let fire of the Holy Spirit burn the camp of the enemy now until they are destroyed.

18. Thanks for victory. In Jesus' name, amen. Selah!

Destroying Demonic Routes

1. In the name of Jesus Christ, we lift a standard against the evil plans of the enemy, and we command that the establishment or coming together of the empire of darkness to be overturn.

2. As we speak, the oracle of God the kingdom of darkness is being demolished.

3. Every plot and demonic routes that have been established to carry destruction to us and our families, we cut you off by the fire of God.

4. As it is in the book Isaiah 59:19, "So shall they fear the name of the LORD from the west, and his glory from the rising of the sun. When the enemy shall come in like a flood, the Spirit of the LORD shall lift up a standard against him."

Lord, let your angels fight our battles.

5. Let the fire of God begin to burn on the path of all demons and witchcraft sent to abort our destiny. In Jesus' name.

6. Let the routes of every witchcraft and demonic spirits become their burying places. In the name of Jesus, destroy them.

7. God, release our angels to continually encamp and monitor every entrance of witchcraft that is fashioned against us and destroy them. In Jesus' name.

8. Let any satanic route constructed against us become dark and slippery, and into the very destruction let them fall. In the name of Jesus.

9. God, reign thunder and lightning, scatter the roads of any witch or warlocks trying to destroy us, and let them fall in every destructive plot against us.

10. We thank you for your word in Psalm 7:1 that said, "O Lord my God, in thee do I put my trust: save me from all of them that persecute me, and deliver me."

11. Let the fire of God be a permanent blockage between us and Satanic traps and demons selah!

12. We release by the power of God, the creator of all things, to find, capture, and destroy every demon assigned to bring us to on expected end. In Jesus' mighty name.

13. God, in the name of your son Jesus Christ, we ask

that you release your fire on all fallen angels that are sent to teach your people to do evil. Let God's people go.

14. Shut the doors of darkness that want to destroy your people. In Jesus' name.

Destroying Satanic Communication Systems

1. Let the communication system of all witches and warlocks burn to ashes by the holy fire of God.
2. We ask that you put fire on every witchcraft networks working against my prosperity. We command you to be dismantled by the blood of Jesus Christ.
3. Burn to ashes the witchcraft communication gadgets set up against our life. In Jesus' name.
4. Computer assigned against our life for evil, melt like wax in the presence of God.
5. All demonic traps and monitoring systems setup to watch us, be destroyed.
6. Confuse the tongue of every witchcraft speaking against our destiny. In Jesus' name.
7. Every evil communication against us falls and dies in the name of Jesus.
8. Release confusion in the midst of our enemies. Let them attack each other continually until they are destroyed.

9. Break their necks by the strike of the sword and destroy them with thy tempest.

10. Cause judgement to come upon them continually, overtake them until they are flattened, and let them attack us no more.

11. "The LORD shall cause thine enemies that rise up against thee to be smitten before thy face: they shall come out against thee one way and flee before thee seven ways" (Deuteronomy 28:7).

12. "And he shall be like a tree planted by the rivers of water, that bringeth forth his fruit in his season; his leaf also shall not wither; and whatsoever he doeth shall prosper" (Psalm 1:3).

Destroying Evil Transportation and Satanic Operations

1. Let the fire from heaven fall and consume the transportation of all demonic assignment against our life and family. In Jesus' name.

2. Cut off their route with the blood of Jesus Christ, and send them back with vengeance against the senders.

3. Let the tempest of God blow against every witchcraft transportation system designed against our life and shatter them. In Jesus' name.

4. Overturn every satanic transportation system

assigned against our life. It shall not prosper in Jesus' name.

5. As the angel of God obstructed Balaam, let every witchcraft transportation be blocked and reversed. Let the witches kill themselves now. In Jesus' name.

6. Every accident we command you to dissolve by the power of the blood of Jesus Christ. We shall live and not die.

7. The word of the Lord is the lamp unto our feet and a light to our path. The sun shall not smite us by day nor the moon by night. My God shall preserve our going out and coming in from this time forth.

8. "No weapon that is formed against thee shall prosper; and every tongue that shall rise against thee in judgment thou shalt condemn. This is the heritage of the servants of the LORD, and their righteousness is of me, saith the LORD" (Isaiah 54:17).

9. Father, in the name of Jesus let fire rain down on the transportations used to carry witchcraft that causes destruction in our life and family.

10. We send the angels of God to go and cut off all routes travelled by evil, satanic, and demonic spirits.

11. Lord, let your Kingdom be established. Overturn

and destroy every transportation of lucifer's angel erected against our life and destiny.

12. We speak to the prince of darkness monitoring this area and we command you to leave the territory because it belongs to the Lord.

13. Let the blood of Jesus Christ put up a standard against you with power and fire.

14. Let your hold be no more. we release the angels of God to chase you, overtake you, and destroy you now. In Jesus' name, amen.

Breaking Down Satanic Altars:

1. "Thou preparest a table before me in the presence of mine enemies: thou anointest my head with oil; my cup runneth over. Surely goodness and mercy shall follow me all the days of my life: and I will dwell in the house of the LORD for ever" (Psalm 23:5-6).

2. All assignments and altars that are working against us, let the heavens send judgment against you now. In the name of Jesus.

3. Evil altars, the day of your judgment is now. God, release your fire. Let them melt like wax in your presence, oh God.

4. Let every altar of witchcraft and familiar spirit be

broken in the name of Jesus.

5. We set the fire of God on every demonic powers that are making sacrifices at every crossroads now, in the name of Jesus.

6. We command that every altar of wickedness constructed against us and our families be broken. In Jesus' name.

7. Let the fire of God fall down and consume every altar of false religion in this country. In the name of Jesus.

8. We disgrace every altar of iniquity in our life by the blood of Jesus.

9. We rebuke the spell of any witchcraft pot from our life and families. In the name of Jesus.

10. Every pot cooking my affairs, the Lord rebuke you. Overturn now. In Jesus' name.

11. Let the altar of witchcraft in our households be burned by the fire of God.

12. Cover our possessions under your wings because we dwell in the secret place of your tabernacle.

13. For you have said in Psalm 91:10, "There shall no evil befall me, neither shall any plague come nigh my dwelling."

14. We stand on that authority, and we declare that every alter setup for demonic and satanic attack on your people be broken.

15. Angels of God, capture and destroy their seeds

so that there will be no continuation of them on earth. In Jesus' name, amen.

War Against Satanic Kingdoms:

1. Oh Lord, let your thunder and hailing fire locate all witches and wizards established against us for total destruction and destroy them.
2. As the wax is melted by fire, let all witchcraft devices caging our life or destiny be burned by fire. Let the east wind scatter their ashes in Jesus' name.
3. All witchcraft banks and strong room holding our blessings and treasures release them now by the power of God. In Jesus' name.
4. Every evil coven calling our name, be destroyed by the fire and blood of Jesus.
5. All witches and warlocks holding our picture or image, be consumed by fire. In the name of Jesus.
6. We command my body, soul, and spirit to come out of every witchcraft trap now. In the name of Jesus.
7. Every area of our life caged by evil and satanic power, be released by fire. In the name of Jesus.
8. Lord, overturn every alter setup to fight against our destiny.
9. And every evil alter burning with anything con-

cerning our life, we release the flood of God'
water against you to drown. In the name of Jesus.

Breaking the Hold of Marine Demons:

1. Every marine spirit present in our life and family,
   be destroyed by fire. In the name of Jesus.
2. We break the backbone of every marine demon
   scheming against our life with the hands of fire. In
   Jesus' name.
3. Every work of marine witchcraft in our life, die
   now by the blood and fire of Jesus Christ.
4. We command all marine spirits of witchcraft that
   have a grip in our life to release your hands from
   our life. In the name of Jesus.
5. We speak to the rivers, caves, seas, and oceans to
   release our blessings and turn back to sender all
   witchcraft attacks originated in them.
6. With authority we bring you to a dry land, and we
   scatter you in the desert places where you will die
   a slow death at the hands of God.
7. We command the fire of God to enter the marine
   world and dry up all the water and burn every satanic trap that has been planted in them to destroy
   our life and family.
8. Lord, let the mighty angels ascend on the marine

world and find and burn the root of evil and demonic operations that are established against your people.

9. Every demon operating from the marine realm, your time is up. We bind you with the chains and the fire of God.

10. Lord, let your voice divide the waters and expose every marine demon working against us in secret. Bring them down.

11. Lord, we ask by your grace that you ride upon the many waters and destroy the foundations of marine strong hold.

12. As you have spoken in the beginning to the heavens and the earth, to all creeping things, and to the rest of creation made from the water, we ask you now, Lord, to speak to our lives.

13. Let your voice open the marine world and shake all satanic entrapment used by evil to hold your people captive.

14. We command all marine demon operation around our life, family, and church to die now. Lord, in the name of Jesus, burn their works and nullify their effects now, amen.

Blinding the Eyes of Demonic Entities:

1. Father, in the name of Jesus Christ, blind every witchcraft eye monitoring our life, family, and business.
2. We plead the blood of Jesus against the spirit of destruction, and we ask you, Lord, to pluck their eyes out by fire. In the name of Jesus.
3. In the secret of your tabernacle, you shall hide us and our head shall be lifted up above all demonic monitoring spirit.
4. Lord, let the arrows of fire reign down and destroy monitoring agents over the affairs of our life. In the name of Jesus, blind them.
5. Let Michael, the archangel of God, war in the heavenly realms and destroy the prince of the air that is monitoring our life now.
6. As we release the word of God with the power and the blood of Jesus, let every astral projection used to monitor our life and family be cut off.
7. We command the angels of God to use their sword of flaming fire and cut the silver cord attached to all those engaged in astral projection and destroy their evil works.
8. Let the eyes of every witchcraft manipulating our marriages, families, bloodlines, and all our affairs be plucked out by fire. In Jesus' name.

9. Every demon monitoring and manipulating our finances, be burned by fire now. In Jesus' name.

10. The evil spirits manipulating our spiritual life, be cut off by the arrow of God's fire. In the name of Jesus.

11. Let every evil mirror used to monitor our life be shattered. Jesus, let your blood reign forever.

12. Lord, dispatch your warrior angels to destroy all night raiders assigned to visit our dwelling, dreams, and possessions at nights.

13. No evil shall befall us neither shall any plague come near my dwelling

14. Block the path travelled by aerial spirits wanting to locate us and destroy their route. In Jesus' name.

Nullify Witchcraft Attacks on My Finances:

1. We are the seed of Abraham. We are blessed. Wealth and riches are in our borders.

2. The Lord became poor so that we can be rich in all areas of life.

3. With the Holy Ghost's fire and the lightening of God, we break the cycle of poverty over our life and families.

4. Lord, we ask through your mercy to break the generational curse of poverty that exists in our

bloodlines.

5. As we walk, enlarge my territories and let our steps be a representation of victory. We cancel all spirit of limitations, in Jesus' name.

6. Let the brass heaven over us roll back and melt like wax.

7. Let the earth bring forth healing herbs and fruits of abundance in our life

8. We command the gates of hell to shout up. We cancel the effect of every evil emanating from the gates of hell against our finances.

9. We command the earth under our feet to produce living herbs and fatness for my prosperity.

10. We are a tree planted by the rivers of water. Whatever we do we must prosper because God is with us.

11. Anything in us supporting demonic influences on our finances, we cut you off. Come out with all your roots. In Jesus' name.

12. All demonic strongholds and witchcraft holding our finances, we command you to release it now. In the name of Jesus Christ.

13. When we decree a thing, it shall come to pass. Let the spirit of witchcraft holding our finances and blessings be released now.

14. All forces assigned against our finances, we break your hold now by the fire of God.

15. Prosperity belongs to us; we walk in victory because nothing will be able to stop God's plan for our life.
16. Every ancestral embargo on my finances, we cut you off by the blood of Jesus Christ.
17. We recover our finances and everything stolen from us by witchcraft because the blessing of Abraham is ours.

Press Against the Throne of Witchcraft:

1. Every throne of witchcraft in our neighbourhoods, be pulled down. In the name of Jesus.
2. By the power and authority, we release the angels of God to destroy every plot of territorial demonic influence in this region.
3. Every high seat of drugs, prostitution, lewdness, sorcery, murder, false teaching, poverty, abortion, and destiny killer, break you down now by the power and blood of Jesus Christ.
4. Let the ground open and swallow every witchcraft throne hiding in the body of Christ. In the name of Jesus.
5. Every flying throne of witchcraft, be cast down in the name of Jesus.
6. Every throne of witchcraft set up against our life, be demolished in the name of Jesus.

7. Let the throne of Jesus Christ be established in every area of our life and this region. In the name of Jesus.

8. Let the thunder of God locate and dismantle the high seat of witchcraft in our household.

9. Every throne that has exalted itself against our life, family, and anything concerning us, we cast you down. In the name of Jesus.

10. Lift up the standard, oh Lord, against the flood that the enemy wants to bring into our life.

11. Overturn the ship of the wicked in the storm and tempest of this awesome power. Let the ocean swallow them up.

12. We send the fire of the Lord in the marine world. We command every high seat of marine demons to burn and melt like wax at the presence of the Lord.

Reflective thoughts and expressions

Personal notes: _____

_____

_____

_____

_____

_____

_____

_____

_____

_____

_____

_____

_____

_____

_____

_____

_____

_____

_____

_____

_____

_____

_____

Section 4:

Angelic Assistance and Assignment Prayers (deeper level)

The angels of God are sent to helps us. These entities are spiritual beings and can destroy the work of demonic kingdoms when commanded by us or God. In this realm, angels have different ranks. For example, based on the nature of this book, we will be focusing on the assistance of some of the archangels to carry out specific functions based on the will or purposes of God.

To you, oh God the creator of all things, blessed be your name through your son, Jesus Christ, our Lord and saviour Selah.

Prayer for Justice and Judgement

1. In the name of Jesus Christ of Nazareth, we ask Raquel the Archangel, the friend of God, the angel of justice, fairness, harmony, and vengeance, to plead our cause this day.
2. Lay your judgement at the root of them that raise up against us.
3. Let the scale of justice measure the injustice that

has been laid against us by evil.

4. Cut the cord and lay your boundaries in the sight of our enemies. Divide them with fire, Selah.

5. Let fairness be our shield. Overturn the table of the deceitfulness. Whip them with vengeance.

6. Recompense them by the judgement of God and report our case to the God of creation.

7. Bring harmony to our life now and dismantle every plot of evil designed to destroy our life and families.

8. We pray the vengeance of God's power will sit at the house of every evil doer that rises up against us. In Jesus' name.

9. Make their prayers become sin. Let their tongue cleave to the top of their mouth until they repent.

10. Let Raquel the Archangel go forth and execute now in the land of the wicked that revolt against us. In Jesus' Name.

Binding the Angels of Darkness

1. Archangel Uriel, as you warn the prophet Noah and give him the instruction on how to build the ark and as you instruct Ezra the prophet and answer all his concern so give us knowledge to overcome the plot of the enemy. In Jesus' name.

2. We pray that the angels of God will watch over

our affairs now.

3. We ask, oh God, that you make us into an instrument of violence against the kingdom of darkness.

4. We plead the blood of Jesus upon our possessions. Send your angels with fire to watch over us.

5. Let the wisdom of God be our guidance and enlighten us now.

6. Remove the spiritual cataract from our eyes now, oh God. Let us see our enemies from far off. Protect us.

7. Assign Uriel to instruct us in the night-time so that our plans can be executed before our enemies are awake. Visit us with instructions. In Jesus' name.

8. The enemy's plans shall be revealed to us now. In Jesus' name, bring them confusion.

9. Let the evils in the kingdom of darkness fight against each other until they are utterly destroyed. In the mighty name of Jesus.

Prayer for Healing

1. Raphael, the angel of knowledge and of healing, we ask in the name of Jesus Christ through His blood that you administer healing to every area of our bodies.

2. As the word of God said in Isaiah 53:5 that by the

stripe of Christ we are healed. We command every sickness in our bodies to die.

3. Oh Lord, assign your angel Raphael to perform the gift of healing in us.

4. We call for the angelic assistance of Raphael to visit every sickness in our bodies and with the divine authority to destroy all demons aligned to the sicknesses.

5. Let judgement come at every root of sickness, and let the fire of God destroy them.

6. We command right now that the demon carrying infirmity to our bodies crash and burn by the wind and fire of God.

7. Raphael, overturn any pot cooking infirmities in our life.

8. It is written in Exodus 23:25 that if we serve you, then you shall bless our bread and our water; and you will take away our sickness. We claim this blessing now.

9. We thank you for the redemption stated in Deuteronomy 7:15 that you will take away from us all sickness: "And will put none of the evil diseases of Egypt, which thou knowest, upon thee; but will lay them upon all of them that hate thee." Based on that promise, we command sickness hiding in our bodies to get out and die.

10. O LORD, rebuke me not in thine anger, neither

chasten me in thy hot displeasure. Have mercy
upon me, O LORD; for I am weak: O LORD, heal
me; for my bones are. vexed. My soul is also sore
vexed: but thou, O LORD, how long? Return, O
LORD, deliver my soul: oh save me for thy mercies' sake. For in death there is no remembrance
of thee: in the grave who shall give thee thanks?
(Psalm 6:1-5)

Prayer of Protection, Advocator, and Heavenly Warfare

1. Archangel Michael, the most beloved of God, the
   protector and advocator of mankind, the leader
   of God's army against all evil forces. You defeat
   Lucifer in the battle of heaven.
2. We call upon you now with the authority of God
   in Christ Jesus that you come to our assistance
   now.
3. You are the lord of warfare in the heaven, and on
   earth the host of God's warriors answer to you.
4. Take control of all spiritual warfare between the
   throne of God and us as you fight and defeat the
   prince of Persia for Daniel. Let the demon block-
   ing our breakthrough die at your hands.
5. We command all demons assigned to abort our
   destiny will burn by the presence of God.

6. Heavenly host, attack and utterly destroy every spirit set out to eat up our blessings.

7. Open the flood gates of heaven and shoot your arrows into every dark area of our life to overturn them.

8. Swing your sword and battle on our behalf. Break down the walls of Jericho that trap us.

9. Now, set us free by the might of your hands as the Lord commands.

10. War, war, war! Breakthrough, now, and flee at the presence of God's army.

11. Pursue them, overtake them, and beat them until they become ashes. Let the east wind scatter them. Let them rise no more.

12. Every hindering spirit, we command you to dry up. God of glory, destroy those that seek after our souls.

13. We war not with flesh and blood and when we command a thing it shall come to pass as it is said in Ephesians 6:12. Satan, we rebuke you from our life, our families, our homes, and all that concerns us. In the mighty name of Jesus.

14. Michael, leader of the army of God, stand guard against every assault of Satan against our life and families.

15. Expose the angel of light in our life.

16. Confuse, dismantle, and chase the evils with fire

hailing stones to break the necks and hands that hold us captive. Fire of God, come now.

Reflective thoughts and expressions

Personal notes: _____

_____

_____

_____

_____

_____

_____

_____

_____

_____

_____

_____

_____

_____

_____

_____

_____

_____

_____

_____

_____

Section 5:

Identifying and Destroying Satanic Strategies

War Against the Prince of Persia

"For thou hast said in thine heart, I will ascend into heaven, I will exalt my throne above the stars of God: I will sit also upon the mount of the congregation, in the sides of the north: I will ascend above the heights of the clouds; I will be like the most High" (Isaiah 14:13-14).

1. You prince of Persia, angel of light, you have lost the battle in heaven. We come against you now by the blood of Jesus and the Archangel Michael, the leader of God's army.

2. We renounce your presence from our life and families. Every plot you have setup, we command all demons you assigned to fall.

3. The powerful blood of Jesus is released against you. Your days are numbered. Be gone from our life and families now.

4. Jehovah, in the name of your son Jesus Christ, let the kingdom of Satan that has been established over our life and families be removed and burned.

5. Cast down all glory of demons exalting them-selves against us.

6. We are joint heir with Christ, therefore, we are sons and daughters of the most high God. We de-cree now that you and all demons working against our destiny be gone and never return.

7. The bond of fire and chariots with God's angel is released against you concerning our life. You are defeated now. In Jesus' name.

The Wall of Jericho

1. As you command the children of Israel to march around the city of Jericho with singing and a shout for seven times, we march around the walls erected by Satan that hold our blessings captive this moment.

2. Let the thunder of God sound, let the lightening flash, make the heavens burst with fire as we sing praises to you, oh Lord.

3. As your foundation begins to shake, we command that every stronghold against us melt.

4. Let the angels of God ascend and descend from our life and families now.

5. May the sound of the host of heaven in agreement with us break your wall now.

6. We decree now, break the walls holding our fi-

nances.

7. Break the wall aborting our destinies!
8. Break the wall destroying our families!
9. Break the wall that blocks the answer from God concerning our life!
10. Break the stronghold of sickness and infirmities in our life and families!
11. Break all generational curses operating in our bloodlines and marriages!
12. Break all negative words spoken against us and our families!
13. Break everything holding me back because of these walls!
14. And as you crash to the ground, we stand on the promises of God. We are above, not below. We are the head, not the tail.
15. We are blessed without measure. We shall receive all good things.
16. We command the east wind to blow and totally scatter the remnants of the wall so that we will not face them again. In Jesus' name, amen.

The Waters

1. Rivers, ponds, springs, seas, and oceans, the Lord God made these. This day, we command that all spirits of witchcraft working through them and

affect our life to drown.

2. Expose them, Lord. Destroy the demons in the marine world working against our life and families.

3. Anything planted in the waters working to abort our destiny, we apply the fire of God to burn you to ashes.

4. We decree every spirit of witchcraft operating in the marine to be cast in the desert. There the spirits will melt like wax in the presence of God.

5. Let the angel of God enter the marine world now and dismantle every trap designed to kill us.

6. Blood of Jesus, enter the marine world and cleanse it. Pour your liquid fire now and burn all demons hiding in the marine world.

The Author's Personal Note

I must always give thanks to the Lord God almighty, through His son Jesus Christ, the saviour and redeemer of our souls from hell. I must also give thanks to my family and friends for their never-ending supporting role in seeing this book through.

I want to thank you for taking the time to read this book. I hope it blesses your soul and transforms your prayer life into a fighting force that will destroy the works of Satan on earth.

To the teachers of the word and leaders in the churches of God, I encourage you all to embrace the power of strategic prayer and teach your congregation how to pray so that they can walk in victory.

Finally, I must thank the production team, marketing, sales distribution outlets, and all who worked on this project for it to be a success. Thank you, again.

From,
Silford Edwards

Reflective thoughts and expressions

Personal notes: _____

_____

_____

_____

_____

_____

_____

_____

_____

_____

_____

_____

_____

_____

_____

_____

_____

_____

_____

_____

_____

_____

About the Author

Silford Edwards has spent many years in the Christendom. His thirst for the will of God to be done on earth has led him to embark upon deeper studies. Because of this, he has been exposed to and has gained significant knowledge in the moves of God, religions, history, and spirituality. These experiences gave him a greater understanding of covenant relationships and what it will take for us to become that which God has ordained to be on earth. Some specific areas of experience are in deliverance ministry, strategic prayer, and worship. Out of these came "The Kingdom Decree."

His belief and expression are that if we build and maintain a covenant relationship with God through Jesus the Christ then we are in a position to determine the directions of our lives and have dominion over the power of darkness. The word of God is His will for our lives. To declare a word and for the word to come to pass, we must first understand it.

Each one of us has within us the potential to have complete authority over the affairs of our lives if we learn and apply the word of God.

Being strategic in our prayer lives requires us to be precise and concise, and the best way to do so is to develop a planned strategy before we start praying. These strategies include, but are not limited to, identifying the cause or problems, find the scriptures that speak to the situation, look at what may cause the situation, and develop the main prayer points to deal with it.

Silford believes that spiritual warfare is more serious than physical war because this is a supernatural power and to be effective or victorious will take deliberate planning and actions to execute the word of God in any situation.

I hope as you read this book you will get a deeper understanding of strategic prayer and how to apply the words of God to your prayer lives to be most effective against the kingdom of darkness.

Printed in the USA
CPSIA information can be obtained
at www.ICGtesting.com
LVHW010556110923
757638LV00006B/122

9 781685 564865